aging

Other Books by Henri J. M. Nouwen

Intimacy
Creative Ministry
With Open Hands
The Wounded Healer
Pray to Live

aging

Henri J. M. Nouwen · Walter J. Gaffney
PHOTOGRAPHS BY RON P. VAN DEN BOSCH

DOUBLEDAY & COMPANY, INC. · GARDEN CITY, NEW YORK · 1974

Library of Congress Cataloging in Publication Data
Nouwen, Henri J M
  Aging.
  Includes bibliographical references.
  1. Aged—Conduct of Life.   I. Gaffney, Walter J.,
1938–   joint author.   II. Title.
BJ1691.N68   170′.202′26
ISBN 0-385-04181-0
Library of Congress Catalog Card Number 74–1773
9 8 7 6 5 4 3 2

*Text Copyright © 1974 by Henri J. M. Nouwen and Walter J.
Gaffney · Photographs by Ron P. van den Bosch Copyright ©
1974 by Ron P. van den Bosch · All Rights Reserved · Printed in
the United States of America*
Designed by Aileen Friedman

Acknowledgments

This book would not have been written without the encouragement, constructive criticism, and secretarial assistance of many friends.

We are grateful, first of all, to Peter Naus and Don McNeill, who made us aware of the great importance of studying and writing about aging and encouraged us to present some of our ideas during a conference at the University of Notre Dame.

We also owe special thanks to Mary Carney, Richard Cockrell, Ed Dobihal, Teresa Geiger, Rufus Lusk, Jeannette Rogers, Brenda Stiers, and Colin Williams for their many suggestions; to the Sisters of Mercy in Madison, Connecticut, for giving us a quiet place to work; and to Shirley Richardson for her excellent secretarial help.

The text, however, represents only a part of the work which went into the making of this book. Our friend Ron van den Bosch, who spent four months with us at the Yale Divinity School, has been able to express with his camera what we were not able to express in words. The many photographs he made during his stay in the United States and during his travels through Holland, Belgium, Northern Ireland, France, West Germany, Czechoslovakia, and Crete, helped us to see aging as a universal experience which, although it has many faces and appearances, transcends the endless variations of being alive.

Henri J. M. Nouwen
Walter J. Gaffney
New Haven

Contents

Prologue: The Wagon Wheel

The Wagon Wheel

This is a book about aging. It is a book for all of us, since we all age and so fulfill the cycle of our lives. This is what the large wagon wheel reclining against the old birch in the white snow teaches us by its simple beauty. No one of its spokes is more important than the others, but together they make the circle full and reveal the hub as the core of its strength. The more we look at it, the more we come to realize that we have only one life cycle to live, and that living it is the source of our greatest joy.

The restful accomplishment of the old wheel tells us the story of life. Entering into the world we are what we are given, and for many years thereafter parents and grandparents, brothers and sisters, friends and lovers keep giving to us—some more, some less, some hesitantly, some generously. When we can finally stand on our own feet, speak our own words, and express our own unique self in work and love, we realize how much is given to us. But while reaching the height of our cycle, and saying with a great sense of confidence, "I really am," we sense that to fulfill our life we now are called to become parents and grandparents, brothers and sisters, teachers, friends, and lovers ourselves, and to give to others, so that, when we leave this world, we can be what we have given.

The wagon wheel reminds us that the pains of growing old are worthwhile. The wheel turns from ground to ground, but not without moving forward. Although we have only one life cycle to live, although it is only a small part of human history which we will cover, to do this gracefully and carefully is our greatest vocation. Indeed we go from dust to dust, we move up to go down, we grow to die, but the first dust does not have to be the same as the second, the going down can become the moving on, and death can be made into our final gift.

Aging is the turning of the wheel, the gradual fulfillment of the life cycle in which receiving matures in giving and living makes dying worthwhile. Aging does not need to be hidden or denied, but can be understood, affirmed, and experienced as a process of growth by which the mystery of life is slowly revealed to us.

It is this sense of hope that we want to strengthen. When aging can be experienced as a growing by giving, not only of mind and heart, but of life itself, then it can become a movement towards the hour when we can say with the author of the Second Letter to Timothy:

As for me, my life is already being poured away as a libation, and the time has come for me to be gone. I have fought the good fight to the end. I have run the race to the finish; I have kept the faith. (2 Tm 4:6–7)[1]

But still—without the presence of old people we might forget that we are aging. The elderly are our prophets, they remind us that what we see so clearly in them is a process in which we all share. Therefore, words about aging may quite well start with words about the elderly. Their lives are full of warnings but also of hopes.

Much has been written about the elderly, about their physical, mental, and spiritual problems, about their need for a good house, good work, and a good friend. Much has been said about the sad situation in which many old people find themselves, and much has been done to try to change this. There is, however, one real danger with this emphasis on the sufferings of the elderly. We might start thinking that becoming old is the same as becoming a problem, that aging is a sad human fate that

nobody can escape and should be avoided at all cost, that growing towards the end of the life cycle is a morbid reality that should only be acknowledged when the signs can no longer be denied. Then all our concerns for the elderly become like almsgiving with a guilty conscience, like friendly gestures to the prisoners of our war against aging.

It is not difficult to see that for many people in our world, becoming old is filled with fear and pain. Millions of the elderly are left alone, and the end of their cycle becomes a source of bitterness and despair. There are many reasons for this situation, and we will try to examine them carefully. But underneath all the explanations we can offer, there is the temptation to make aging into the problem of the elderly and to deny our basic human solidarity in this most human process. Maybe we have been trying hard to silence the voices of those who remind us of our own destiny and have become our sharpest critics by their very presence. Thus our first and most important task is to help the elderly become our teachers again and to restore the broken connections among the generations.

We want to speak, therefore, first of all, about the elderly as our teachers, as the ones who tell us about the dangers as well as the possibilities in becoming old. They will be able to show us that aging is not only a way to darkness but also a way to light. Secondly, we want to speak about aging and care in order to show not just how we can take care of elderly people, but more, how we can allow the elderly to cure us of our separatist tendencies and bring us into a closer and more intimate contact with our own aging.

We believe that aging is the most common human experience which overarches the human community as a rainbow of promises. It is an experience so profoundly human that it breaks through the artificial boundaries between childhood and adulthood, and between adulthood and old age. It is so filled with promises that it can lead us to discover more and more of life's treasures. We believe that aging is not a reason for despair but a basis for hope, not a slow decaying but a gradual maturing, not a fate to be undergone but a chance to be embraced.

We therefore hope that those who are old, as well as those who care, will find each other in the common experience of aging, out of which healing and new life can come forth.

Part One: Aging

Introduction

An old Balinese legend might help us to think more clearly about our own society and the way we relate to those we have labeled "the old" or "the elderly."

It is said that once upon a time the people of a remote mountain village used to sacrifice and eat their old men. A day came when there was not a single old man left, and the traditions were lost. They wanted to build a great house for the meetings of the assembly, but when they came to look at the tree-trunks that had been cut for that purpose no one could tell the top from the bottom: if the timber were placed the wrong way up, it would set off a series of disasters. A young man said that if they promised never to eat the old men any more, he would be able to find a solution. They promised. He brought his grandfather, whom he had hidden; and the old man taught the community to tell top from bottom.[2]

Is it true that in our days we too sacrifice the old, ostracize them and expel them from the community of the living? Have we also lost the traditions which helped us to understand our own lives and now can no longer tell top from bottom?

There indeed is little doubt that for many people growing old is a way to destruction and darkness. But there are many others—maybe hidden by their young friends or made strangers by our own fears—for whom growing in years is growing to the light and who are keeping alive for us the art of telling top from bottom in the midst of our fragmented existence.

Therefore, we will first look at aging as a way to the darkness. Then we hope to discover how aging is or can become a way to the light.

Aging As a Way to the Darkness

The well-known French author Simone de Beauvoir has published an impressive and well-documented study of aging. After a long and detailed analysis of the biological, ethnological, historical, and phenomenological aspects of aging, she concludes: ". . . The vast majority of mankind looks upon the coming of old age with sorrow or rebellion. It fills them with more aversion than death itself."[3] It seems as if the pessimistic and depressing mood which pervades her view of old age is a contemporary reflection of the complaint expressed so many years ago in the Thirty-first Psalm. There an old man says:

Take pity on me, Yahweh,
  I am in trouble now.
Grief wastes away my eye,
  my throat, my inmost parts.

For my life is worn out with sorrow,
  my years with sighs;
my strength yields under misery,
  my bones are wasting away.
I am contemptible,
  Loathsome to my neighbours,
to my friends a thing of fear.

Those who see me in the street
  hurry past me;
I am forgotten, as good as dead in their hearts,
  something discarded. (Psalm 31:9–12)

"Something discarded"—that is what too many old men and women have become today. Of the twenty million people in the United States who are sixty-five or older, nearly seven million are living below the poverty level or are too poor to afford necessary medical .expenses. Many of the twenty-four thousand nursing homes, in which one million elderly people live, are so overcrowded and understaffed that real cure or even care is practically impossible. The median income for an aged man is less than half of that for the total population, and of the aged women who earn any income at all, half bring home less than one thousand dollars a year. Sometimes those who must enter homes for the elderly have to sign all their possessions over for life to those in charge. Sharon Curtin was surely right when she remarked: "It is a full-time, job to be old and poor."[4] Yet we Americans spend at least five billion dollars a year on gadgets, cosmetics and techniques to prevent us from looking old, whereas during 1970 only three hundred and thirty million dollars were made available to those who were really old.[5]

So it is not surprising that many elderly people can say with the Psalmist: "Those who see me in the street hurry past me; I am forgotten,

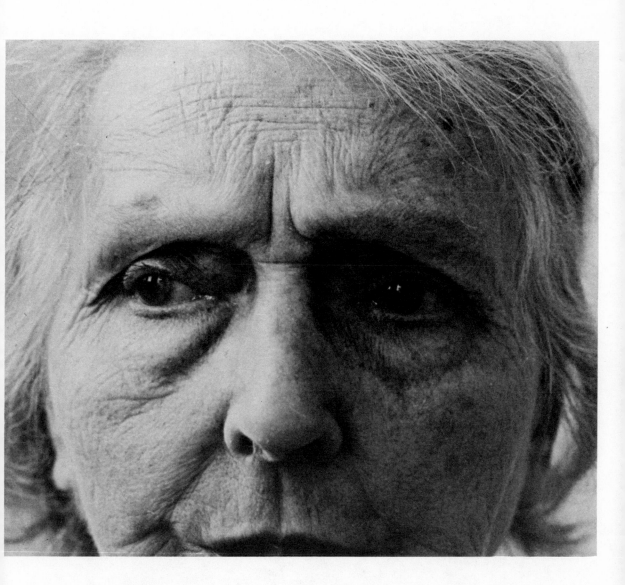

as good as dead in their hearts, something discarded." Our society does not have room for the elderly. They are ostracized, excommunicated, expelled like contagious lepers, no longer considered as full members of the human community. Perhaps this occurs more subtly than in previous times, but the result is the same. Simone de Beauvoir is correct when she says that old age, for many, is far more fearful than death. We cannot imagine a state beyond our existence on this earth, but we can anticipate the pains of excommunication in old age. Waiting for torture about which we know is endlessly more frightening than waiting for the departure from life about which we do not know. This is what eighty-two-year-old Florida Scott-Maxwell meant when she wrote:

We wonder how much older we have to become, and what degree of decay we may have to endure. We keep whispering to ourselves, "Is this age yet? How far must I go?" For age can be dreaded more than death . . . It is waiting for death that wears us down, and the distaste for what we may become.[6]

We cannot deny these facts and feelings. We even have to enter them and ask ourselves: "What is it that makes many old people feel ostracized?" In light of this question we can examine at least three factors: segregation, desolation, and loss of self. We could consider these factors as three forms of rejection: rejection by society, rejection by friends, and rejection by our inner self.

Segregation

Claire Townsend describes old age as the last segregation. This seems a very appropriate expression in a civilization in which "being" is, in fact, considered less important than "doing" and "having." Our desire to acquire a job, to make a good career, to have a house, a car, money, stocks and bonds, good relations, and a certain amount of knowledge, has become so central in our motivation to live that he or she who no longer is able to relate to the world in those "desirable" terms has become a stranger.

This might also explain some of the problems related to volunteer work. Although many elderly have acquired, often through hard work, enough money to have safe old years, they still tend to feel less valuable when they no longer can earn their own living. Frequently they experience volunteer work as a second-rate activity. Just as wealthy students sometimes resist volunteer work and prefer a "real paying job," so many elderly feel that they are only acceptable members of society when they get paid for what they do. It indeed is a strange paradox that in a culture which creates more and more free time, "volunteerism" carries little prestige with it. But there are exceptions. We know a man who had saved enough in his late forties to retire, and now spends his time as a volunteer in a large city hospital, offering his help to people who otherwise would have received little attention. His desire was not to acquire

more, but to keep doing something useful. For him the value of doing was no longer dependent on acquiring. And there are many similar examples of impressive volunteerism.

But the sad fact remains that many people start experiencing themselves as old when certain institutional arrangements, such as mandatory retirement, place them outside the circle of those who identify themselves primarily with what they do, have, or can acquire. Those who can no longer participate in this "exciting" rivalry and competition (in which human values have been degraded to numbers on a scoreboard) are doomed to experience themselves as less than human. Indeed, they don't count any longer. They become the sad fallout of our society, the pitiful long-distance runners who run out of breath. Sharon Curtin, a young woman who has worked with the elderly, remarks:

I have learned that a culture which equates material possessions with success, and views the frantic, compulsive consumer as the perfect citizen, can afford little space for the aged human being. They are past competing, they are out of the game. We live in a culture which endorses what has been called "human obsolescence." After adolescence, obsolescence. To the junk heap, the nursing home, the retirement village, the "Last Resort."[7]

The fear of becoming old in our Western world is, for the most part, determined by the fear of not being able to live up to the expectations of an environment in which you are what you can produce, achieve, have, and keep. Therefore, those who are forced by retirement laws to give up their desire for more property and more power are looked down upon as having passed the line of productivity. They are tolerated but no longer taken seriously. In a society where the basic interest is in profit, old age in general cannot be honored because real honor would undermine the system of priorities that keep this society running.

So segregation takes place in every situation in which "being" becomes subordinated to "having." Perhaps this explains why those few powerful people who are trying to escape the destiny of segregation can only do so by clinging desperately to their property, power, and influence, thus choosing the role of oppressor instead of the oppressed. When we see how powerful old people in church and state often anxiously hold on to outdated viewpoints and old-fashioned customs, thereby preventing real growth and development, we may wonder if, in fact, they are not simply clinging to the only acceptable form of self-identification left to them in our achievement-oriented world. In this way, they are as much victims of old age as their less fortunate contemporaries.

It is important to repeat that this segregation often takes place in very subtle forms. Children write polite letters to their grandparents, but they

write only what they think their grandparents want to hear. Younger people visit older people but seldom make them part of their lives, since they do not want to hurt, upset, or shock them. Arguments are prevented, the truth hidden, and much of human reality kept out of sight. All this happens with the good intention of offering the old father, mother, aunt, uncle, or friend an undisturbed last phase of life. But, in fact, their lives become less human, less full, and less real because, consciously or unconsciously, they have been forced into the prison of a selective communication which prevents them from seeing, understanding, and interpreting their own world as it is. Florida Scott-Maxwell writes:

We live in a limbo of our own. Our world narrows, its steady narrowing is constant pain. Friends die, others move away, some become too frail to receive us, and I become too frail to travel to them . . . Letters can be scarce so we tend to live in a world of our own making, citizens of Age, but otherwise stateless.[8]

We should add here that this segregation, in overt as well as in covert forms, is often strengthened by inhibiting forms of self-segregation. Often we settle, relatively early in life, into clear-cut patterns of thinking and behaving, which make us feel secure and protected. We close ourselves off from the possibilities of new life styles which might challenge us to take risks and to change. And so a certain decreased level of awareness already starts long before we reach old age and makes us very vulnerable to rejection by others when our self-constructed, comfortable life style no longer works.

Thus, segregation, which is rejection by our society, and more often than not is strengthened by self-rejection, becomes one of the most powerful factors in making many of the elderly feel like unwanted hangers-on.

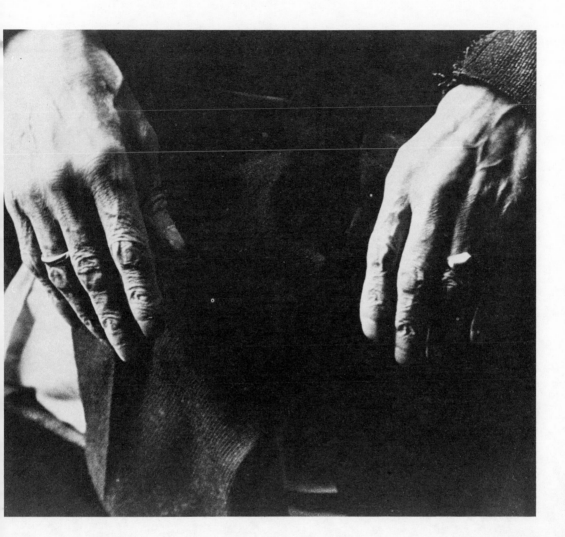

Desolation

Although segregation is one of the most important elements in the predicament of the elderly, only a few of them will be consciously aware of
its destructive dynamics. In talking about their sadness and sufferings,
desolation, not segregation, is uppermost in their minds. /Desolation is
the crippling experience of the shrinking circle of friends with the dev-
astating awareness that the few years left to live will not allow you to
widen the circle again. /Desolation is the gnawing feeling of being left
behind by those who have been close and dear to you during the many
years of life. It is the knowledge of the heart saying that nobody else
will be as close to you as the friend you have lost, because a friend is
like wine: "When it grows old, you drink it with pleasure." (Si 9:10)
You have only one life cycle to live and only a few really entered that
cycle and became your travel companions, sharing the moments of ecstasy

and despair, as well as the long days of routine living. When they leave you, you know you have to travel on alone. Even to the friendly people you will meet on your way, you will never be able to say, "Do you remember?", because they were not there when you lived it. Then life becomes like a series of reflections in a broken window.

Often it is believed that it is isolation that makes old age so hard to live through. But isolation only means less social contact as compared with others, and many people can be very content with only a few relationships. Desolation, however, is less social contact as compared to previous years in one's life.[9] It means a rupture in one's history, a cutting away of familiar ties, a social denudation. In this desolation the experience of loneliness breaks through to the center of one's existence, a loneliness often expressed in fond memories of the time when one was still together with friends and relatives.

If segregation is rejection by society, desolation is often experienced as a "rejection" by one's friends. Although there might be many explanations for the fact that husband, wife, or friend died before we did, our heart often responds with feelings of rejection and sometimes even anger, because we have been left behind and alone in a harsh and pitiless society. These feelings are often so deeply hidden that they are seldom expressed to others or to oneself, but they are, by that fact, no less real and painful.

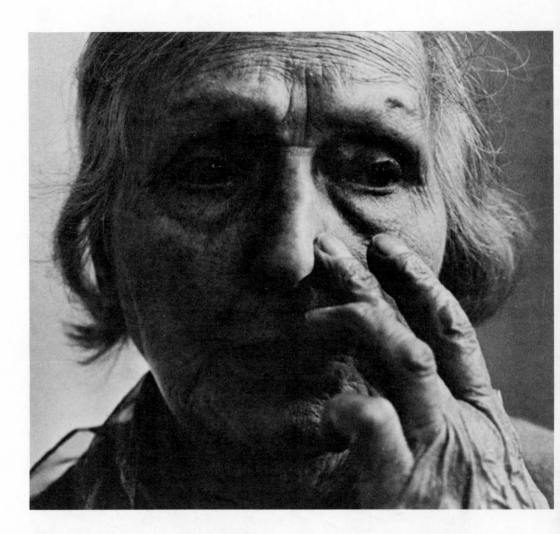

The Loss of Self

Segregation and desolation are powerful factors which create a severe alienation in the elderly. But one way of rejection, which is, in the final analysis, probably the most destructive, is self-rejection. This is the inner ostracism by which the elderly not only feel they are no longer welcome in the society of profit, or able to keep their small circle of intimate friends together, but by which they also feel stripped of their own feeling of self-worth and no longer at home in their most inner life. The loss of self, although closely related to segregation and desolation, is still a separate factor in the predicament of many elderly. It calls for special attention.

He who has lost his most inner self has nothing left to live for. He can say with Ben Sira in the Old Testament:

"O death, your sentence is welcome
to a man in want, whose strength is failing,
to a man worn out with age, worried about everything,
disaffected and beyond endurance." Si 41:3–4)

Maybe the loss of self becomes most visible in those whose whole identity is absorbed by the past, who hardly have any satisfaction in the present, and who look into the future as into a thickening darkness. There can hardly be a more alienating feeling than that which believes, "I am who I was." This preoccupation with the past, as Robert N. Butler has observed, imprisons old people in anxiety, guilt, despair, and depression.[10] They become victims of a society which identifies their humanity with their productivity, and prisoners of others who made them believe that their self-worth was determined by their friends. In this way they lose their inner freedom and have no room for a creative response to their loneliness. They are doomed to sourness, bitterness, and cynicism; their future can be nothing else than emptiness, darkness, and hell.

When people have lost their own "self," they are without hope. Segregation and desolation have robbed them of their center. They have opened the innermost room of their sanctuary and allowed the evil forces to take possession of it. This is not just theoretical speculation. There *are* old people for whom there is only darkness. In that darkness no color can be seen, no sign can be discovered, no one can be trusted. This darkness can be filled with resentment, anger, jealousy, and, sometimes, violent rage. There is a powerful theme in human history from the Dark Ages to Shakespeare and from Shakespeare's *Macbeth* to Polanski's *Rosemary's Baby,* telling us that indeed old men and women can become warlocks and witches—ugly, ill-tempered creatures who cast a dangerous spell on people and spread a contagious fear wherever they go.

The heavy pessimism pervading Simone de Beauvoir's study, the depressive statistics about the later years of life, and the all-too-visible rejection of the elderly through segregation, desolation, and the loss of self, make it indeed very difficult to see growing old other than as a way to darkness. Quite often one gets the feeling of being caught in a diabolical circle in which darkness can perhaps be temporarily denied, but which seems to be the inescapable destiny of everyone who calls himself or herself young.

This diabolical circle of darkness is most vividly expressed in the Greek story of an old Spartan man. This man was segregated by his community, had lost his friends, and had interiorized his rejection to such a degree that he took destiny into his own hands, left the village, and went off to the hills to die. But before he left, his grandson was asked by his son to offer the old man a blanket which could keep him warm during his last hours. But the grandson cut the blanket in two so that half would be available for his own father when he grew old enough to die.[11]

This story portrays the inescapable darkness of old age, in whose shadow grandfather, son, and grandson will be consumed and where love can only be an act of blind heroism and old age a period of silent despair.

In Sparta the old went off into the hills to die; in Bali they were sacrificed by their own people. Today the excommunication continues, perhaps with more sophisticated means, but nonetheless with the same destructive result.

Is this where we have to stop and bow our heads in sadness? We do not believe so, because once in a while a young man might come into our world and tell us that he has hidden the old man who can tell us top from bottom and prevent our assembly house from caving in on us. It is this young man who may unmask the myths about growing old and remind us that aging can indeed also be a way to the light.

Aging As a Way to the Light

There is no doubt that much of the darkness we have described is related to structural cankers in our society which prevent healing for many elderly persons. And although we have become painfully aware of our social predicament, it is beyond the scope of this book, and also beyond our competence, to offer solutions for these obvious structural defects. We even have to say that, in all likelihood, many of the conditions which are the cause of much suffering to the elderly will remain with us for some years to come.

But it would be a temptation to allow the darkness to overwhelm us and make us insensitive to the signs of light which become visible in the lives of many old people. In the midst of all the darkness we have described, it is possible to suddenly come across an old man with a soft smile, suggesting that maybe there is more to see than we first imagined.

Now in Jerusalem there was a man named Simeon. He was an upright and devout man; he looked forward to Israel's comforting and the Holy Spirit rested on him. It had been revealed to him by the Holy Spirit that he would not see death until he had set eyes on the Christ of the Lord. Prompted by the Spirit he came to the Temple; and when the parents brought in the child Jesus to do for him what the law required, he took him into his arms and blessed God; and he said:

"Now, Master, you can let your servant go in peace, just as you promised; because my eyes have seen the salvation which you have prepared for all the nations to see, a light to enlighten the pagans and the glory of your people Israel." (Lk 2:25–32)

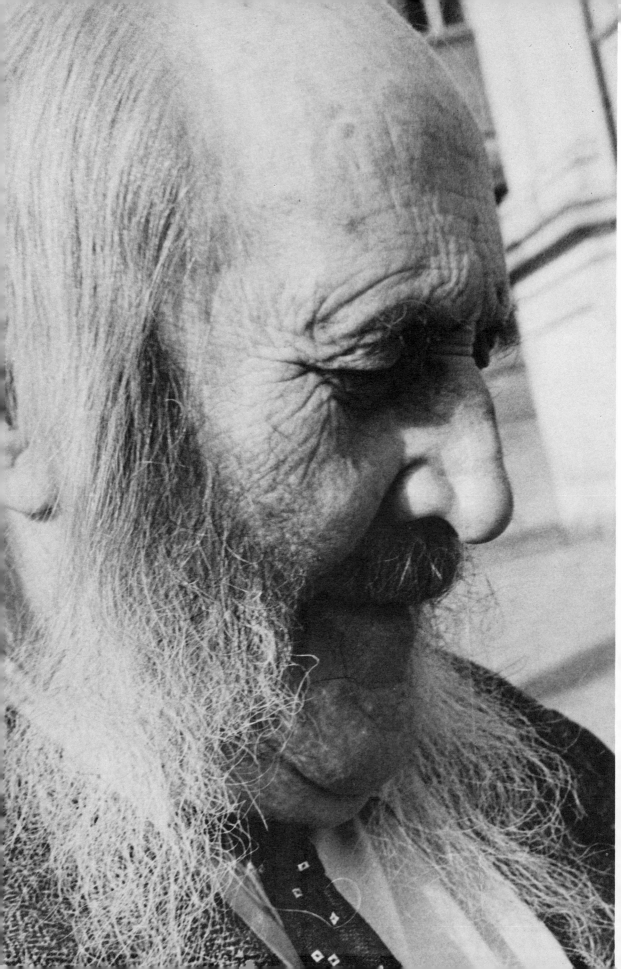

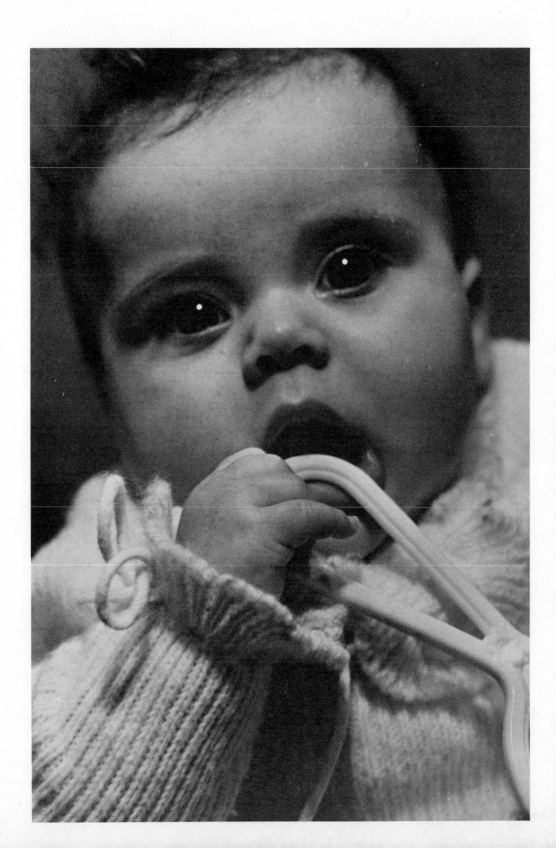

Simeon breaks through our pessimism, and his blessing is like a gentle smile in the face of our depressive statistics. He looks at us as if to say: "Have you ever thought that coming of age might also be the way to light?" And Simeon might be able to open our eyes for new visions and new sounds. Then we can hear the Psalmist saying:

The virtuous . . . will flourish in the courts of our God, still bearing fruit in old age, still remaining fresh and green, to proclaim that Yahweh is righteous. . . . (Ps 92:13–15)

As your word O Yahweh unfolds, it gives light, and the simple understand. (Ps 119:130)

Moses, who had seen this light growing in the virtuous, tells his people: "Ask . . . of your elders, let them enlighten you." (Dt 32:7) So maybe, after all, there are old men and women hidden from our troubled vision, whom we have to bring into the midst of our assembly so that they can cast away the darkness of our confusing existence and tell us top from bottom.

"Ask of your elders, let them enlighten you." Do we see them in our midst? They are there, but statistics, surveys, and questionnaires seldom reveal them to us. The darkness of old age has been pretty well documented, but the light does not seem to fit into the computers and tabulation machines of the profit-makers. However, concerned people today are beginning to dispel the mythological aspects of growing old. They are convinced that much of the fear of becoming old in young and middle-aged people is based more on rumors than on facts. A study by Dr. Alexander Leaf for *National Geographic* beautifully portrays the graceful elderly in Russia, Kashmir and Ecuador.[12] And Bernice Neugarten has recently completed a long-term study of more than two thousand persons between the ages of seventy and seventy-nine.[13] She demonstrates convincingly that old age is not just the gray shadowy end of the life cycle in which we slowly lose our best self. Stereotyping the elderly has, in fact, created unnecessary fear of aging and causes "negative or hostile attitudes between age groups."[14] Stereotypes lead to separations between the generations. Neugarten writes: "So long as we believe that old people are poor, isolated, sick and unhappy (or, to the contrary, powerful, rigid and reactionary), we find the prospect of old age particularly unattractive. We can then separate ourselves comfortably from older persons and relegate them to inferior status.[15] The resulting harm is great. Younger people shy away from close contact with the elderly, and the elderly no longer can be the teachers of the young by bringing them in touch with their own aging and helping them discover the precious sensitive center of their creativity. Much violence in our society is based on the illusion of immortality, which is the illusion that life is a property to be defended and not a gift to be shared. When the elderly

no longer can bring us in contact with our own aging, we quickly start playing dangerous power games to uphold the illusion of being ageless and immortal. Then, not only will the wisdom of the elderly remain hidden from us, but the elderly themselves will lose their own deepest understanding of life. For who can remain a teacher when there are no students willing to learn?

But the elderly are not necessarily the gloomy, inarticulate, dependent group of our society. In fact, in many old people we will find more differentiation, uniqueness, and special talents than in the young. "People do differ; they also become increasingly different over time as each person accumulates an idiosyncratic set of experiences and becomes committed to an unique set of people, things, interests and activities . . . Increased differentiation occurs over the life cycle."[16]

When we are able to cast off our fears and come close to the many who have grown old, we see old men and women telling stories to children

with eyes full of wonder and amazement. We think of old Pope John giving life to an old church, and of old Mother Teresa offering hope to the sick and dying in India. We look at the last self-portrait of Rembrandt and discover a depth that was not there before. We marvel at the last works of Michelangelo and realize they are his best. We remember the strong face of the old Schweitzer, the piercing eyes of the elderly Einstein, and the mild face of Pope Pius X. We recognize the transparency of the farmer looking over his fields in which he has worked for many years, the deep understanding smile of the woman who saw her own children die long before she did, and the concentrated expression on the face of the old poet. We hear people talking about the old country, the olden days, and old friends, as if their pains and joys had composed a melody that is growing to a silent climax. Then we know that slowly but surely, in the broken, beaten faces of the many who belabored the world for years and years, a new light has become visible—a light that cannot die because it is born out of growing old.

As we reflected on our personal experiences, one of us remembered his grandmother in Holland.

When I think of her I do not feel sad or depressed—rather a warm smile dawns on the horizons of my thoughts. I see her beautiful white hair and her small tender face which felt so soft every time she kissed me. Sitting in her easy chair, she listened with great attention to all the stories I had to tell about my father and mother, my brothers and sister, my studies and ordination, my plans and my hopes. And I knew for sure she was always on my side. When I complained about my teachers, she made me feel that I was right. When I talked about the long trips I had to make, she usually said: "O poor boy." When I told her how terribly busy I was, she was ready to become angry at anyone who could possibly be blamed. Whatever I said, she would always take it seriously. And although she seldom talked about her long past of eighty years, I saw in her eyes the slow life on a small Dutch farm. I saw the man she met and lived with for forty-five years, and their eleven children. I saw how she taught my father to walk, talk, and go his own way. I saw her endless, frightening asthmatic attacks. I saw her behind the window, looking at the hearse parked in front of the house, provoking a last memory of her husband being carried to his grave. Then again I saw her knitting and knitting and knitting—sweaters and long scarves for me and all her grandchildren. And sitting in front of me with the rosary in her hands, she said: "It was so nice that you annointed me, that was very beautiful. I think I am ready to go." And with a smile she added: "But Henri, you did such a good job I might have to stay a little longer to say more rosaries for the children. And that will keep me quite busy because you know there are quite a few." Then— one day, sitting in her chair behind the window, with her old prayerbook in her hands, she simply bowed her head and left us. And her face was full of peace and light.

Aging *can* be the way to the light. Aldous Huxley knew this when he wrote his brother Julian on his birthday:

It is hard to feel old . . . We both, I think, belong to that fortunate minority of human beings, who retain the mental openness and elasticity of youth, while being able to enjoy the fruits of an already long experience.[17]

We first had to enter into the difficult question: "What makes many old people experience themselves as ostracized?" We now have to ask: "What makes those about whom Huxley speaks grow to their age as to the light?" The second question is more difficult than the first, since in human life pain always seems easier to understand than happiness. Just as we talk easier and more articulately about our legs when they hurt

than when they function well, we spend more time and energy discussing the pains of aging than its possible joys. But when we want to be the children of the light, we have to try to come close to that mysterious gift hidden by the elderly who did not become the victims of rejection. They are more numerous than the "nay-sayers" would have us believe. For example, the elderly Florida Scott-Maxwell informs us:

Age puzzles me. I thought it was a quiet time. My seventies were interesting, and fairly serene, but my eighties are passionate. I grow more intense as I age. To my own surprise I burst out with hot conviction.[18]

Is it possible to describe the full maturity of old age and to capture some of the light radiating from those who experience the days of their old age as precious gifts? It certainly is not easy, but maybe we can come close by speaking of the hope, the humor, and the vision of the many who have grown old gracefully and carefully.

Hope

One way of describing the way to the light is to call it a slow conversion from wishes to hope. You wish "that," you hope "in." Wishes have concrete objects such as cars, houses, promotions, and wealth. Hope is open-ended, built on the trust that the other will fulfill his or her promises. Hope is like the sound of a church bell moving over a snow-covered land. A marriage built on wishes is in constant danger, but a marriage built on hope is open-ended and full of possibilities, since it is the partners themselves who count and not what they can do or have.

Therefore, the conversion from wishes to hope asks for a slow process of disengagement in which we are willing to detach ourselves from many little and big things of the moment and open our arms to the future. Robert Kastenbaum has rightly emphasized that this conversion does not take place when someone is labeled "old" by society. The disengagement,

which makes hope possible, "requires a changed perception of time and death around mid-life."[19] C. G. Jung was well aware of the importance of this time of the life cycle.

The noon of life is the moment of greatest deployment, when a man is devoted entirely to his work, with all his ability and all his will. But it is also the moment when the twilight is born: the second half of life is beginning . . . At midday the descent begins, determining a reversal of all the values and all the ideals of the morning.[20]

Every time life asks us to give up a desire, to change our direction, or redefine our goals; every time we lose a friend, break a relationship, or start a new plan, we are invited to widen our perspectives and to touch, under the superficial waves of our daily wishes, the deeper currents of hope. Every time we are jolted by life, we are "faced with the need to make new departures."[21] But if this does not happen in the early years, how can we expect that it will come about later?

When hope grows we slowly see that we are worth not only what we achieve but what we are, that what life might lose in use, it may win in meaning. This is beautifully expressed in an old Taoist parable which tells us about a carpenter and his apprentice who saw a huge oak tree, very old and very gnarled.

The carpenter said to his apprentice: "Do you know why this tree is so big and so old?"
The apprentice said: "No . . . Why?"
Then the carpenter answered: "Because it is useless. If it were useful it would have been cut down, sawed up and used for beds and tables and chairs. But, because it is useless, it has been allowed to grow. That is why it is now so great that you can rest in its shadow."

When the value of the tree became the tree itself, it was free to grow to the light. That is the power of hope.

Humor

The way to the light is a hopeful way and therefore full of humor. Humor is knowledge with a soft smile. It takes distance but not with cynicism, it relativizes but does not ridicule, it creates space but does not leave you alone. Old people often fill the house with good humor, and make the serious businessman, all caught up in his great projects, sit down and laugh. Knowledge with a soft smile is a great gift. One day an important, highly decorated diplomat knelt down before Pope John, kissed his ring and said: "Thank you, Holy Father, for that beautiful encyclical *Pacem in Terris* which you gave the world." Pope John looked at him with a smile and answered: "Oh, did you read it too?" And when someone asked him: "How many people work in the Vatican?", he thought for a while and then said: "Well, I guess about half of them."

Humor is a great virtue, because it makes you take yourself and your world seriously, but never too much. It brings death into every moment of life, not as a morbid intruder, but as a gentle reminder of the contingency of things.

All over the globe, old people who have a sense of humor can play the most beautiful games with our overly serious world. In Amsterdam, old ladies sent baskets with food and drink by way of a long cable to the students who had occupied a university building, and enjoyed fooling the police, who took their task with a seriousness as if they had to save the world. In Venice, California, old men and women sit on the benches along the beach and chat for hours with long-haired, barefoot hippies, with liberated gay people, and with self-made gurus, yogis, and meditators. And in Ecuador a 123-year-old man, asked about women, burst out in laughter and said: "I can't see them too well any more, but by feeling I can tell if they are women or not." These old people have broken through the many barriers which have kept people separated by fear and suspicion and are able to appreciate the many new attempts to live a liberated life. Sometimes old people radiate a deep understanding that says: "I know what you young people are trying to do—I know it very well. Just keep trying. It is worth it, because I know how it feels to be free." And when they look at you, you see a light that shines far beyond the eyes of their wrinkled faces.

One of us remembers an elderly woman who lived on the first floor of his tenement when he was a young boy.

She was the happiest person I ever knew. Yet hardship was no stranger to her. She had lost her husband years before, her income was very meager, and her eyesight was failing. But she brought up her children and remained joyful toward life. Whenever I failed to stop in to see her after school she would say: "Walter, I missed you today." How I loved to visit her apartment. It was filled with cats, fish, birds, turtles, and a dog named "Ginger." Every child on the block had a personal interest in them and she loved to have the children in. One day I asked her: "How can you keep track of all these animals?" She smiled and said: "I love to care for living things. They are a constant reminder of the beauty of life." She showed that love of life every night when she would sit on her porch and warmly greet everyone who passed by. Her favorite saying was, "Happy-go-lucky"—and she was. My playmates and I learned from her a life-long lesson—aging was not only tolerable but fun. She died a few years ago in her eighties, and those of us who knew her and loved her said: "She sure died 'happy-go-lucky.'"

Perhaps it is detachment, a gentle "letting-go," that allows the elderly to break through the illusions of immortality and smile at all the urgencies and emergencies of their past life. When everything is put in its proper place, there is time to greet the true reasons for living.

Vision

Hope and humor can give rise to a new vision. Once in a while we meet an old man or woman looking far beyond the boundaries of their human existence into a light that seems to embrace him or her with gentleness and kindness. Once in a while we hear about this light as about a friendly host calling us home. When Florida Scott-Maxwell describes her life in old age, we start seeing how aging can become a growing vision of the light. She writes:

A long life makes me feel nearer truth, yet it won't go into words, so how can I convey it? I can't, and I want to. I want to tell people approaching and perhaps fearing age that it is a time of discovery. If they say—"Of what?" I can only answer, "We must each find out for ourselves, otherwise it won't be discovery.[22]

The vision which grows in aging can lead us beyond the limitations of our human self. It is a vision that makes us not only detach ourselves from preoccupation with the past but also from the importance of the present. It is a vision that invites us to a total, fearless surrender in which the distinction between life and death slowly loses its pain.

This is most sensitively expressed by Aldous Huxley in his description of the death of his first wife, Maria. With his hand on Maria's head, he softly speaks to her:

Let go, let go . . . go forward into the light. Let yourself be carried into the light. No memories, no regrets, no looking back-wards, no apprehensive thoughts about your own or anyone else's future. Only light. Only this pure being, this love, this joy.[23]

Can we say anything more? Yes, we think we can, because we have the feeling that, whereas humor might be able to create a communication that breaks through the boundaries between young and old, travelers and dwellers, hosts and guests, the light might dissolve much deeper separations and bring all humanity into a liberating unity.

This awareness is most vividly expressed by the Dutch priest Han Fortmann. While traveling in India he discovered that he was suffering from a lethal cancer and had to go home to die. On his deathbed he was able to write, while his strength was slowly fading away, these beautiful words:

I proceed from the simple irrefutable fact that in the crucial moments of life . . . (such as death), even though people come from diverging cultures and religions, they find that same essen-

tial word: Light! For isn't it true? There must be a basic similarity between the Enlightenment spoken of by the Hindus and Buddhists and the Eternal Light of the Christians. Both die into the Light. One practical difference could well be that the Buddhist, more than the contemporary Christian, has learned to live with the light (nirvana) as a reality long before he dies. . . . That interior participation, that Enlightenment, intended "for every man who comes into the world"—as John's gospel puts it—has received far less attention in practical preaching than in the teaching of Satori in Zen Buddhism or Samadi in Hinduism. But whoever has once met God no longer finds the hereafter question interesting. Whoever has learned to live in the Great Light is no longer worried by the problem of whether the Light will still be there tomorrow . . . The need to pose skeptical questions about the hereafter seems to disappear as the divine Light again becomes a reality in everyday life, as it is meant to, of course, in all religions.[24]

These words, written by a dying man, reveal the nearly overwhelming vision that aging can be a growing into the light, the light which takes away all the dark and gray lines that divide religious cultures and people and unites all the colors of the human search into one all-embracing rainbow. It is this vision of the light that may grow in our lives as we are coming of age and may make a narrowing path into a widening avenue.

Hope, humor, and vision: these three factors can create those fortunate human beings who are able to retain mental openness, "while enjoying the fruits of an already long experience." The old Simeon in the temple of Jerusalem definitely belonged to those fortunate people. Not unlike the old Balinese grandfather, brought to the assembly to tell top from bottom, Simeon was led to proclaim the light, prepared for all the nations to see, by a small child laid in his arms. And so young and old embrace each other in the realization that maybe, after all, old age is not the "last segregation" but the last illusion, since it is revealed to us that ultimately we are not divided between young and old, but united as children of the light.

Conclusion

Is aging a way to the darkness or a way to the light? It is not given to anyone to make a final judgment, since the answer can only be brought forth from the center of our being. No one can decide for anyone else how his or her aging shall or should be. It belongs to the greatness of men and women that the meaning of their existence escapes the power of calculations and predictions. Ultimately, it can only be discovered and affirmed in the freedom of the heart. There we are able to decide between segregation and unity, between desolation and hope, between loss of self and a new, recreating vision. Everyone will age and die, but this knowledge has no inherent direction. It can be destructive as well as creative, oppressive as well as liberating.

What seems the most frightening period of life, marked by excommunication and rejection, might turn into the most joyful opportunity to tell our community top from bottom. But who is the one who is going to call the elderly from their hiding places? Who is the one who will take their fear away and will lead them out of the darkness of segregation, desolation, and loss of selfhood into the light which is prepared for all the nations to see? Who is that young man who will have the courage to step forward in his society and proclaim that by ostracizing the old men the traditions will be lost and a series of disasters could take place?

It is the one who cares. Through caring, aging can become the way to the light and offer hope *and* new life.

Part Two: Caring

Introduction

A story told by Oskar Kokoschka, about his visit to a London museum, can help us reach a better understanding of caring in the context of aging.

I was in England during World War I, moneyless and miserable. My wife, who is younger and more courageous than I am, said: "Let's go to a museum for relief." There was destruction in the whole world. Not only were bombs being dropped on London—but every day we heard of another city being destroyed. Devastation, ruins, the annihilation of a world becoming poorer and sadder. That was bitter. I looked at Rembrandt's last self-portrait: so hideous and broken; so horrible and hopeless; and so wonderfully painted. All at once it came to me: to be able to look at one's fading self in the mirror—see nothing—and paint oneself as the néant, the nothingness of man! What a miracle, what an image! In that I found courage and new youth. "Holy Rembrandt," I said. Indeed, I owe my life only to the artists.[25]

There can hardly be a better image of caring than that of the artist who brings new life to people by his honest and fearless self-portrait. Rembrandt painted his sixty-three self-portraits not just as "a model for studies in expression" but as "a search for the spiritual through the channel of his innermost personality."[26] Rembrandt felt that he had to enter into his own self, into his dark cellars as well as into his light rooms, if he really wanted to penetrate the mystery of man's interiority. Rembrandt realized that what is most personal is most universal. While growing in age he was more and more able to touch the core of the human experience, in which individuals in their misery can recognize themselves and find "courage and new youth." We will never be able to really care if we are not willing to paint and repaint constantly our self-portrait, not as a morbid self-preoccupation, but as a service to those who are searching for some light in the midst of the darkness.

To care one must offer one's own vulnerable self to others as a source of healing. To care for the aging, therefore, means first of all to enter into close contact with your own aging self, to sense your own time, and to experience the movements of your own life cycle. From this aging self, healing can come forth and others can be invited to cast off the paralyzing fear for their future. As long as we think that caring means only being nice and friendly to old people, paying them a visit, bringing them a flower or offering them a ride, we are apt to forget how much more important it is for us to be willing and able to be present to those we care for. And how can we be fully present to the elderly when we are hiding from our own aging? How can we listen to their pains when their stories open wounds in us that we are trying to cover up? How can we offer companionship when we want to keep our own aging self out of the room, and how can we gently touch the vulnerable spots in old people's lives when we have armored our own vulnerable self with fear and blindness? Only as we enter into solidarity with the aging and speak out of common experience, can we help others to discover the freedom of old age. By welcoming the elderly into our aging self we can be good hosts and healing can take place. Therefore, when speaking about caring in the context of aging, we want to speak first about caring as the way to the self before we speak about caring as the way to others.

Caring As a Way to the Self

Our first question is not how to go out and help the elderly, but how to allow the elderly to enter into the center of our own lives, how to create the space where they can be heard and listened to from within with careful attention. Quite often our concern to preach, teach, or cure prevents us from perceiving and receiving what those we care for have to offer. Does not healing, first of all, take place by the restoration of a sense of self-worth? But how can that take place unless there is someone able to discover the beauty of the other and willing to receive it as a precious gift? Where else do we realize that we are valuable people except in the eyes of those who by their care affirm our own best self?

To receive the elderly into our inner self, however, is far from easy. Old age is hidden not just from our eyes, but much more from our feelings. In our deepest self we keep living with the illusion that we will always be the same. We not only tend to deny the real existence of old men and women living in their closed rooms and nursing homes, but also the old man or woman who is slowly awakening in our own center. They are strangers, and strangers are fearful. They are intruders threatening to rob us of what we consider our own.

Not too long ago a thirty-two-year-old, good-looking, intelligent man, full of desire to live a creative life, was asked: "Jim, what are your plans for the future?" And when he answered: "I want to work with the elderly and I am reading and studying to make myself ready for that task," they looked at him with amazement and puzzlement. Someone said: "But Jim, don't you have anything else to do?" Another suggested: "Why don't you work with the young? You'll really be great with them." Another excused him more or less, saying: "Well, I guess you have a problem which prevents you from pursuing your own career." Reflecting on these responses, Jim said: "Some people make me feel as if I have become interested in a lost cause, but I wonder if my interest and concern do not touch off in others a fear they are not ready to confront, the fear of becoming an old stranger themselves."

Thus care for the elderly means, first of all, to make ourselves available to the experience of becoming old. Only he who has recognized the relativity of his own life can bring a smile to the face of a man who feels the closeness of death. In that sense, caring is first a way to our own aging self, where we can find the healing powers for all those who share in the human condition. No guest will ever feel welcome when his host is not at home in his own house. No old man or woman will ever feel free to reveal his or her hidden anxieties or deepest desires when they only trigger off uneasy feelings in those who are trying to listen. It is no secret that many of our suggestions, advice, admonitions, and good words are often offered in order to keep distance rather than to allow closeness. When we are primarily concerned with giving old people something to do, offering them entertainment and distractions, we might avoid the painful realization that most people do not want to be distracted but heard, not entertained but sustained.

An old lady once told the following story:

I was so happy when one day a nice young student came to visit me and we had such a marvelous time. I told her about my husband and my children and how lonely and sad I often feel. And when I was talking, tears came out of my eyes, but inside I felt glad that someone was listening. But then—a few days later the student came back to me and said: "I have thought a lot about what you told me and about how lonely you feel . . . and I have thought about what I could do to help you . . . and I wonder if you might be interested in joining this club that we are having . . ." When I heard her saying this I felt a little ashamed, since I had caused so many worries for this good person, whereas the only thing I wanted was someone to listen and to understand.

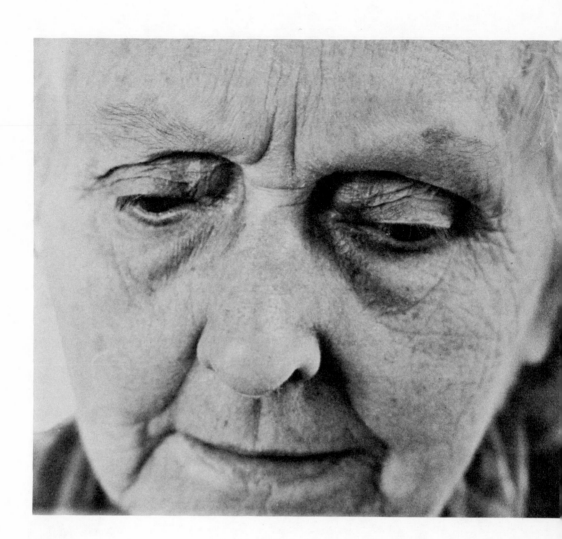

Although old people need a lot of very practical help, more significant
to them is someone who offers his or her own aging self as the source of
their care. When we have allowed an old man or woman to come alive in
the center of our own experience, when we have recognized him or her
in our own aging self, we might then be able to paint our self-portrait in a
way that can be healing to those in distress. As long as the old remain
strangers, caring can hardly be meaningful. The old stranger must first
become part of our inner self and a welcome friend who feels at home in
our own house.

What, then, are the characteristics of a caring person, of someone
whose care brought him in contact with his own self? There are obviously
many, but two seem most important here: poverty and compassion. Let
us have a closer look at both of them.

Poverty

Poverty is the quality of the heart which makes us relate to life, not as property to be defended but as a gift to be shared. Poverty is the constant willingness to say good-by to yesterday and move forward to new, unknown experiences. Poverty is the inner understanding that the hours, days, weeks, and years do not belong to us but are the gentle reminders of our call to give, not only love and work, but life itself, to those who follow us and will take our place./He or she who cares is invited to be poor, to strip himself or herself from the illusions of ownership and to create some room for the person looking for a place to rest. The paradox of care is that poverty makes a good host. When our hands, heads, and hearts are filled with worries, concerns, and preoccupations, there can hardly be any place left for the stranger to feel at home.

We can experience this quite literally when we enter a room of a counselor, minister, or teacher, in which walls, tables, and chairs are so covered with books that we can hardly imagine that our own personal concerns can still be perceived as worth listening to. Such a place is like a New York street in which so many cars are idling that nobody can move, in which the automobile itself has stopped all mobility. Such a place is literally "pre-occupied."

Therefore, to create space for the elderly means, first of all, that I myself must stop relating to my life as to an inalienable property I am obliged to defend at all cost. How can I ever allow the aged to enter into my world when I refuse to perceive my life as a fleeting reality I can enjoy but never grasp, as a precious gift I can foster but never cling to? How can I make any old person feel welcome in my presence when I want to hold on to my life as to a possession that nobody can take away from me? How can I create a friendly space for the elderly when I do not want to be reminded of my own historicity and mortality, which make me just as much a "passer-by" as anybody else?

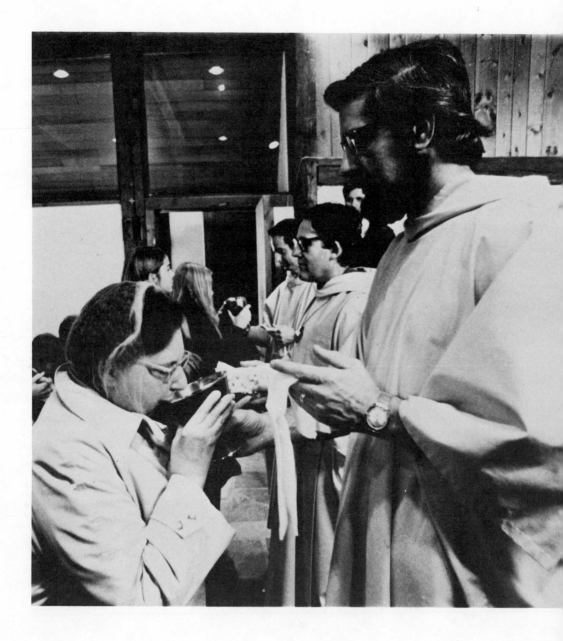

To care for the elderly means then that we allow the elderly to make us poor by inviting us to give up the illusion that we created our own life and that nothing and nobody can take it away from us. This poverty, which is an inner detachment, can make us free to receive the old stranger into our lives and make that person into a most intimate friend.

When care has made us poor by detaching us from the illusion of immortality, we can really become present to the elderly. We can then listen to what they say without worrying about how we answer. We can pay attention to what they have to offer without being concerned about what we can give. We can see what they are in themselves without wondering what we can be for them. When we have emptied ourselves of false occupations and preoccupations, we can offer free space to old strangers, where not only bread and wine but also the story of life can be shared.

Compassion

In a poor heart compassion can grow, because in a poor heart the pains of growing old can be recognized and shared. Compassion is the second most important characteristic of caring, since it allows us to overcome the fear of old strangers and invite them as guests into the center of our own intimacy. When we have taken away the artificial and often defensive distinctions between young and old, we will be able to share the common burdens of aging. Then those who care and those who are cared for no longer have to relate to each other as the strong to the weak, but both can grow in their capacity to be human.

Compassion makes us see beauty in the midst of misery, hope in the center of pain. It makes us discover flowers between barbed wire and a soft spot in a frozen field. Compassion makes us notice the balding head and the decaying teeth, feel the weakening handgrip and the wrinkling skin, and sense the fading memories and slipping thoughts, not as a proof of the absurdity of life, but as a gentle reminder that "unless a wheat grain falls on the ground and dies, it remains only a single grain, but if it dies, it yields a rich harvest." (John 12:24) Compassion makes us break through the distance of pity and bring our human vulnerabilities into a healing closeness to our aging brother and sister. Compassion does not take away the pains and the agonies of growing old, but offers the place where weaknesses can be transformed into strengths. Compassion heals because it brings us together in patience, that is, in a purifying waiting for the fulfillment of our lives.

So compassion is the quality of the human heart that makes it possible for people of very different ages and life styles to meet each other and to form community. Thomas Merton describes compassion as the purifying desert in which we are stripped of all our false differences and enabled to embrace each other as the children of the same God. He says:

There is no wilderness so terrible, so beautiful, so arid and fruitful as the wilderness of compassion. It is the only desert that shall truly flourish like the lily . . .[27]

It is this compassion that can make us live many lives, the lives of the young as well as the lives of the old. Someone once said: "You live as many lives as you speak languages." That is true because every time we allow another person into our desert and learn to speak his or her language, we live our lives together and deepen each other's humanity. And have we ever fully realized how rich the language of the elderly really is?

Poverty and compassion are the two main qualities of those who care. They are the essentials of our self-portrait, which we have to keep painting if we expect to be healers to those we encounter in the midst of their despair and confusion. Let us now see how this healing can take place.

Caring As a Way to the Other

Caring can lead to a new self-understanding, but this self-understanding can never be its own goal. We are for others. Therefore we are called to put our aging self at the service of the aging other. The challenge of care for the elderly is that we are called to make our own aging self the main instrument of our healing.

It seems important, however, to say that caring for the aging is not a special type of care. As soon as we start thinking about care for the aging as a subject of specialization, we are falling into the trap of societal segregation, which care is precisely trying to overcome. When we allow our world to be divided into young, middle-aged, and old people, each calling for a specialized approach, then we are taking the real care out of caring, since the development and growth of men and women take place, first of all, by creative interaction among the generations. Grandparents, parents, children, and grandchildren—they all make the whole of our life cycle visible and tangible to us at every moment of our lives. They offer a healing expectation as well as a healing memory. We expect to be like father and grandfather, and we remember being like son and grandson. And so expectations and memories touch each other and make it possible to live the whole of life at every moment of our existence. That is the core of all caring: to be always present to each other. Caring is the way to the other by which a healing community becomes possible.

It is very sad to realize how difficult this creative interaction among the generations has become. When we see how many new university campuses are being erected in the middle of deserts or cornfields, we become painfully aware of the counter-educational effects of isolation among generations. In these new "halls of learning," thousands of students are packed together, and their sheer numbers make meaningful contact with their teachers practically impossible. Numerous students spend most of their four years of college education almost exclusively with their peers, unable to play with a child, work with a teen-ager, talk with an adult, or have any human contact with the elderly. Those who are separated in order to be educated find themselves in a situation in which the educating context of life is taken away from them. Being in close contact with peers during your formative years is extremely valuable, but when there is no world around you as a reminder of where you came from and where you will go, that closeness might become stagnating instead of mobilizing. And that is a real tragedy.

Therefore, caring for the aged asks for a life style in which the generations are brought into contact with each other in a creative and re-creative way. Those who are in touch with their own aging self might be able to offer the ground where grandfathers and grandmothers, fathers and mothers, sons and daughters, grandsons and granddaughters can come and work together to bring forth the fruits of the earth which are given to them.

Having stressed that caring for the aging other is not a special type of care, we would now like to describe the two main characteristics of caring as the way to others: acceptance and confrontation.

Acceptance

What does caring mean when we think of the many people for whom growing old has become a way to the darkness? What is there to say to men and women who feel forgotten and lonely, and who are approaching death as the only way to escape their misery? How do we listen when there are no words of joyous memories, happy events, and a growing light? How do we respond to those who feel that all their fears, but none of their hopes, have been fulfilled?

There are no easy answers to these questions. There does not seem to be a right reaction or response that fits the occasion. The mystery of a failing life is too deep to grasp. But perhaps, while looking into the tired and despairing eyes of the elderly, we might see what Isaiah saw:

Without beauty, without majesty (we saw him),
no looks to attract our eyes;
a thing despised and rejected by men,
a man of sorrows and familiar with suffering,
a man to make people screen their faces;
he was despised and we took no account of him.
And yet ours were the sufferings he bore,
ours the sorrows he carried. (Is 53:2–4)

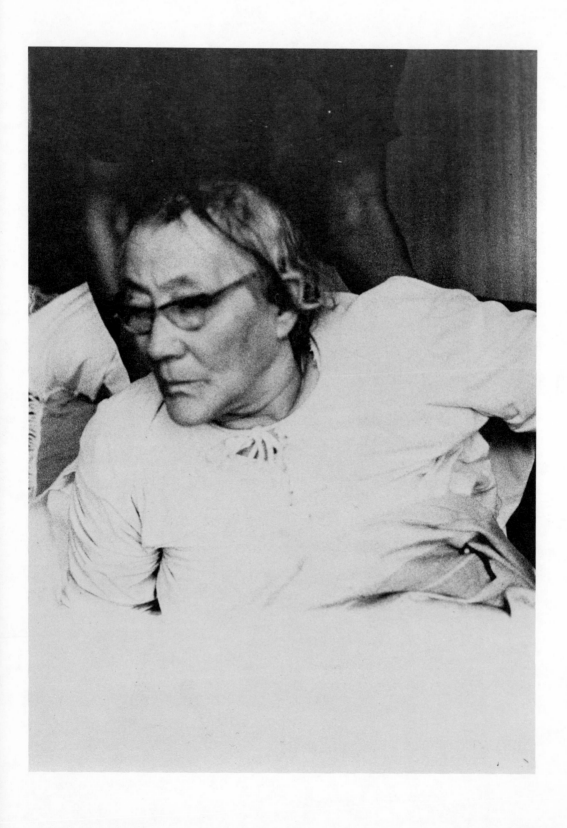

Indeed, it is our world which is reflected in the eyes of the old, miserable man. Ours are the sufferings he bore, ours the sorrows he carried.

The painful suffering of many old people which makes their aging into a way to the darkness cannot be understood by pointing to their mistakes, weaknesses, or sins. By doing so we might avoid the realization that the fate of many old people reflects an evil that is the evil of a society in which love has been overruled by power, and generosity by competition. They are not just suffering for themselves but for all of us who are, knowingly or unknowingly, responsible for their condition.

What can we say to the many who have become the outcasts of our cruel society? Maybe only that for us who care, their misery can become a warning mirror in which we can see our own greedy faces. Yet for those who suffer, the rejection by their society can lead to the recognition of an acceptance we ourselves have not been able to give. Out of the recognition that life is determined neither by what one did, had, or achieved, nor by one's friends or relatives, nor even by one's own self-understanding, the way might be found to Him whose heart is greater than ours and who says through His own son, the broken servant of Yahweh: "You are accepted."

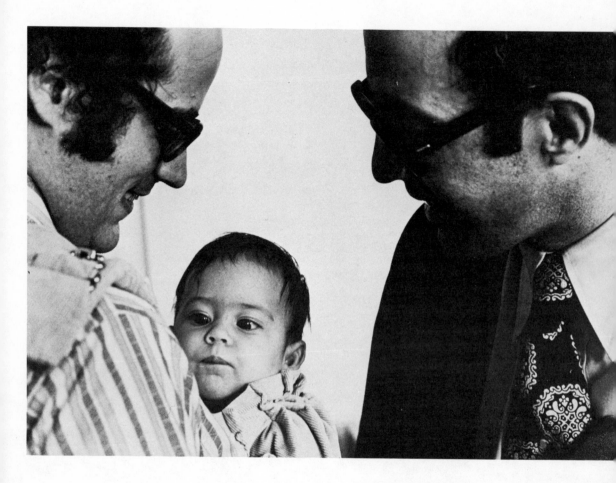

In the honest and painful recognition of human rejection God's acceptance can be affirmed. It does not make sense to point to little consoling events in the past which can be held on to. It does not make sense to say: "Yes, I see you are miserable, but look at your happy children, the people you helped and the things you left behind." That only increases guilt feelings and denies the reality of the experience of failure. The only hope is in the simple fact that someone who dares to listen and to face the failing of life in its naked reality, will not run away but say with a word, a touch, a smile or friendly silence: "I know—you had only one life to live and it cannot be lived again, but I am here with you and I care." Maybe in the midst of this darkness, God's acceptance can be felt through the gentle touch of the one who cares and allows the miserable stranger into his own home.

Confrontation

Acceptance is crucial for many elderly people, but it should not be understood as a passive agreement with the facts of life. On the contrary, care is more than helping people to accept their fate. Real care includes confrontation. Care for the aging, after all, means care for all ages, since all human beings—whether they are ten, thirty, fifty, seventy, or eighty years old—are participating in the same process of aging. Therefore, care for the aging means, more often than not, confronting all men and women with their illusion of immortality out of which the rejection of old age comes forth.

It is indeed the task of everyone who cares to prevent people—young, middle-aged, and old—from clinging to false expectations and from building their lives on false suppositions. If it is true that people age the way they live, our first task is to help people discover life styles in which "being" is not identified with "having," self-esteem does not depend on success, and goodness is not the same as popularity. Care for the aging means a persistent refusal to attach any kind of ultimate significance to grades, degrees, positions, promotions, or rewards, and the courageous effort to keep men and women in contact with their inner self, where they can experience their own solitude and silence as potential recipients of the light. When one has not discovered and experienced the light that is love, peace, forgiveness, gentleness, kindness, and deep joy in the early years, how can one expect to recognize it in old age? As the book of Sirach says: "If you have gathered nothing in your youth, how can you find anything in your old age?" (Si 25:3–4) That is true not only of money and material goods, but also of peace and purity of heart.

Confrontation, by which room is created to allow the eternal light to break into the darkness, is the radical side of care, because it promotes a risky detachment from the concerns of the world and a free manifestation of that love which can change the shape of our society. It not only unmasks the illusions but also makes visible the healing light that gives us the "power to become children of God."

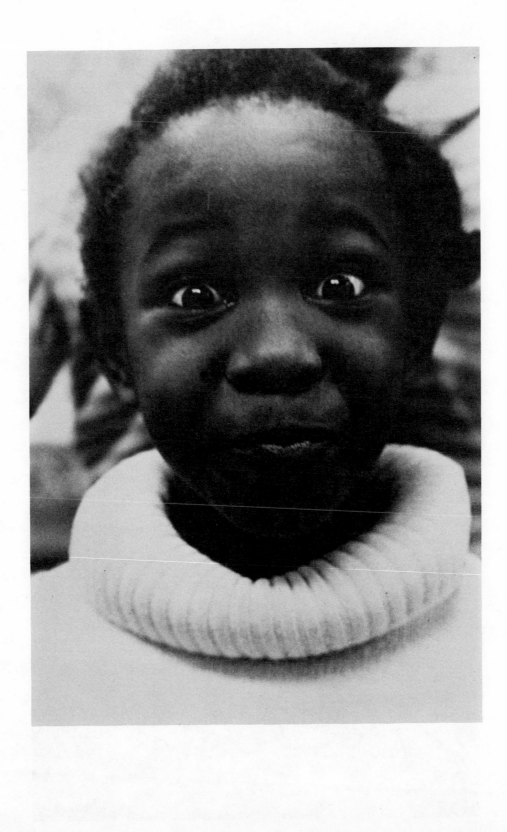

Both acceptance and confrontation belong to the healing care of the aging. Rembrandt not only looked at his own brokenness. He also confronted the people who saw his self-portrait with their own illusions, creating the possibility for the healing light to touch them in their innermost selves.

Conclusion

We started our discussion of care with the story of Oskar Kokoschka, who experienced healing by looking at Rembrandt's honest self-portrait. We want to conclude with a story about another painter, Asher Lev, a young Jewish boy from Brooklyn who experienced acceptance and confrontation in the words of his caring father.

In Chaim Potok's book *My Name Is Asher Lev*, this young painter says about himself:

I drew . . . the way my father looked at a bird lying on its side against the curb near our house.
"Is it dead, Papa?" I was six and could not bring myself to look at it.
"Yes," I heard him say in a sad and distant way.
"Why did it die?"
"Everything that lives must die."
"Everything?"
"Yes."
"You too Papa? And Mama?"
"Yes."
"And me?"
"Yes," he said. Then he added in Yiddish, "But may it be only after you live a long and good life, my Asher."

*I could not grasp it. I forced myself to look at the bird. Every-
thing alive would one day be as still as that bird?*
"Why?" I asked.
*"That's the way the Ribbono Shel Olom made His world,
Asher."*
"Why?"
*"So life would be precious, Asher. Something that is yours for-
ever is never precious!"*[28]

The care of the old for the young is no different from the care of the
young for the old. Real care takes place when we are no longer separated
by the walls of fear, but have found each other on the common ground of
the human condition, which is mortal but, therefore, very very precious.

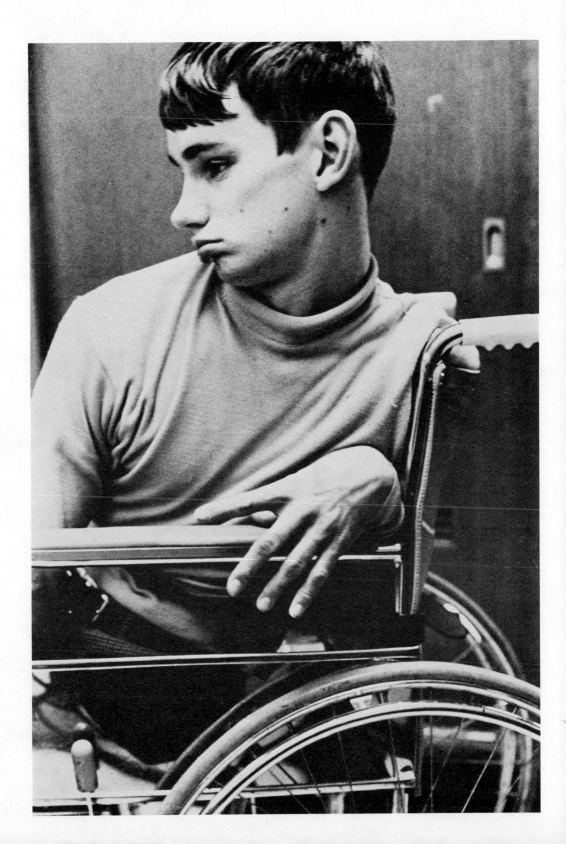

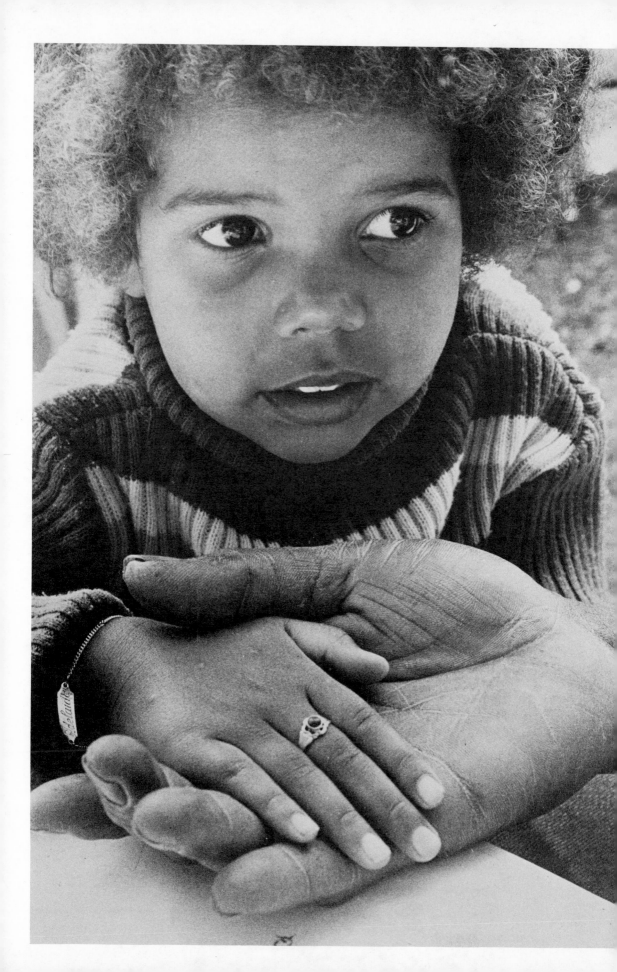

Epilogue: The Wagon Wheel

The Wagon Wheel

This is a book about aging, about the common human destiny of becoming old. Many things have not been mentioned. We did not speak about the housing and health problems of the elderly or about their need for meaningful activity and communication. We limited ourselves to a reflection on our basic human attitudes towards aging in the hope of developing an inner criterion to distinguish between reactions which only reinforce our own prejudices and responses which free the elderly as well as ourselves.

The main conviction underlying all of what we have been trying to say is that we will never be able to give what we cannot receive. Jesus did not multiply bread before he had received five loaves from the boy in the crowd which he wanted to help. Only when we are able to receive the elderly as our teachers will it be possible to offer the help they are looking for. As long as we continue to divide the world into the strong and the weak, the helpers and the helped, the givers and the receivers, the independent and the dependent, real care will not be possible, because then we keep broadening the dividing lines that caused the suffering of the elderly in the first place.

Just as the greatest gift to the East is to allow the East to change the West, the most important contribution to the elderly is to offer them a chance to bring us into a creative contact with our own aging. Just as the handicapped should remind us of our limitations; the blind, our lack of vision; the anxiety-ridden, our fears; and the poor, our poverty—so the old should remind us of our aging. Thus we can be brought in touch with the fullness of the life experience by an inner solidarity with all human suffering and all human growth. This inner solidarity is the basis of the human community where real care and healing can take place. Therefore we entered into the darkness so that we might come to the light, and we spoke about the aging self to come to a fuller care of the aging others.

Aging is one of the most essential human processes, one that can be denied only with great harm. Every man and woman who has discovered or rediscovered his or her own aging has a unique opportunity to enrich the quality of his or her own life and that of every fellow human being.

The wagon wheel reclining against the birch tree in the white snow told us about the fulfillment of the life cycle. But who of us knows when the spokes of our lives have made their full turn? Who knows when we have aged enough to come to the quiet rest which teaches the passer-by? The mystery of life is indeed that we do not decide about our own fulfillment. We never know when we have made the full round. For some it is when they are enjoying the full light of popularity; for others, when they have been totally forgotten; for some, when they have reached the peak of their strength; for others, when they feel powerless and weak; for some it is when their creativity is in full bloom; for others, when they have lost all confidence in their potential. The wheel turns, but we will never know when it is going to stop.

We know one thing, however. For the Son of Man the wheel stopped when he had lost everything: his power to speak and to heal, his sense of success and influence, his disciples and friends—even his God. When he was nailed against the tree, robbed of all human dignity, he knew that he had aged enough, and said: "It is fulfilled." (John 19:30) But the dead body of Jesus has become the sign of hope and new life for many who bear their aging lives in patience. And passing by they say: "In truth, this man was a son of God." (Mark 15:39) The Son of Man grew into the fullness of the Son of God. He was the light that came into our darkness, and revealed to us that the turning of the wheel is not a return to the old ground, but one step forward in the history of our salvation. Every human being has only one life cycle to live, but together our aging can become the fulfillment of the promise of him who by his aging and death brought new life to this world.

Notes

[1] All biblical quotes are from *The Jerusalem Bible,* Alexander Jones, General Editor (Garden City, New York: Doubleday & Company, Inc., 1966).

[2] Simone de Beauvoir, *The Coming of Age* (New York: C. P. Putnam's Sons, 1972), p. 77.

[3] Ibid., p. 539.

[4] Sharon R. Curtin, *Nobody Ever Died of Old Age* (Boston and Toronto: Little, Brown and Company, 1972), p. 56.

[5] Cf. Ralph Nader's Study Group Report on Nursing Homes, *Old Age: The Last Segregation,* by Claire Townsend, Project Director (New York: Bantam Books, 1971).

[6] Florida Scott-Maxwell, *The Measure of My Days* (New York: Alfred A. Knopf, 1968), p. 138.

[7] Curtin, op. cit., pp. 195–96.

[8] Scott-Maxwell, op. cit., p. 137.

[9] Cf. P. Townsend, "Isolation, Desolation and Loneliness," in Ethel Shanas, et al., *Old People in Three Industrial Societies* (New York: Atherton Press, 1965), pp. 255–307; also Peter Naus, "The Impact of Social Factors on Behavior and Well-Being of Elderly People" (Unpublished Study), p. 6.

[10] Cf. Robert N. Butler, "Age: The Life Review," in *Psychology Today,* December 1971, pp. 49–51, 89.

[11] Cf. David Schonfield, Family Life Education Study, "The Later Adult Years," in *The Gerontologist,* Vol. 10, No. 2, Summer 1970, p. 117.

[12] Cf. Dr. Alexander Leaf and John Launois, "Every Day Is a Gift When You Are Over 100," in *National Geographic,* Vol. 143, No. 1, January 1973, pp. 93–118.

[13] Bernice Neugarten, "Grow Old Along With Me! The Best Is Yet To Be," in *Psychology Today,* December 1971, pp. 45–48, 79–81.

[14] Neugarten, op. cit., p. 46.

[15] Neugarten, op. cit., p. 46.

[16] Neugarten, op. cit., p. 48.

[17] Laura Huxley, *This Timeless Moment* (New York: Farrar, Straus & Giroux, 1968), p. 28.

[18] Scott-Maxwell, op. cit., p. 13.

[19] Robert Kastenbaum, "Theories of Human Aging: The Search for a Conceptual Framework," in *The Journal of Social Issues*, October 1965, XXI, No. 4, p. 33.

[20] C. G. Jung, *Modern Man in Search of a Soul*, quoted in Paul Tournier's, *Learn to Grow Old* (New York: Harper & Row, Publishers, 1972), p. 12.

[21] Paul Tournier, op. cit., p. 35.

[22] Scott-Maxwell, op. cit., p. 142.

[23] Huxley, op. cit., p. 25.

[24] Han Fortmann, *Discovery of the East: Reflections on a New Culture* (Notre Dame, Indiana: Fides Publishers, Inc., 1971), pp. 98–99.

[25] Horst Gerson, *Rembrandt Paintings* (New York: Reynal and Company, 1968), p. 478.

[26] Gerson, op. cit., p. 460.

[27] Thomas Merton, *The Sign of Jonas* (Garden City, New York: Doubleday & Company, Inc., 1953), p. 323.

[28] Chaim Potok, *My Name Is Asher Lev* (New York: Alfred A. Knopf: 1972), p. 156.